The 7 Laws of Coaching

Powerful Coaching Skills that will Predict Your Team's Success

FREE BONUS E-BOOK!

Developing Powerful Visions And Inspiring People With Them

Learn how to inspire others with a clear and compelling vision. Understand how to bring your vision to life, and use the wisdom that every great leader has used to help their followers build, maintain and grow their vision into a success!

shapleighpublishing.com/DevelopingPowerfulVisionsBook

Table Of Contents

Introduction

I want to thank you and congratulate you for purchasing the book, The 7 Laws of Coaching.

This book contains proven steps and strategies on how to become a highly effective coach, make the most of your relationship with team members, and thrive as a leader with your team. People respond to genuine leadership and integrity. This book will show you how to establish these qualities with people you're coaching.

Every coach is a great leader while being so much more than that at the same time. A coach is a leader who is followed willingly, without having to drag people along. In order to be this type of leader, there are some guidelines you must adhere to. That's what the 7 Laws of Coaching are all about!

Thanks again for purchasing this book. I hope you enjoy it!

Law One- Getting Into the Right Mindset

Being an effective coach is all about having the appropriate mindset. The attitude you bring to this pursuit plays a role in every aspect of the experience of leadership, from how well team members listen to you, to being able to motivate them, to the level of respect they will show you when you express your authority.

Without the appropriate mental state for coaching, you will not be successful. People respond to what you put forth, even when it's nonverbal. This means being aware of the quality of your presence.

The Definition of Coaching:

Coaching is the method employed for contributing to the development of people's natural abilities and skills and improving performance. It also helps to deal with identifying issues and potential challenges before they turn into huge problems.

Coaches are qualified people who are assigned with helping people reach their full potential for performance. They may be hired by organizations or by individuals needing guidance. An effective coach must ensure that goals are clearly set, expectations are discussed, and ideal achievements are decided together.

A Great Coach is all of These Things:

- **A source of inspiration:**

  Coaches are aware of how to ignite passion and motivate people. They have an energy that is contagious and know exactly how to get their team excited. They can identify and play up each person's unique strengths as well as provide pointers for how best to direct those strengths. A great leader can be counted on to always inspire and motivate and to show others how to discover these qualities within themselves.

- **A trusted guide:**

  An effective coach doesn't have to demand without explanation to get things done and accomplish goals. An inspiring leader instead guides the existing talent in members of his team. He recognizes greatness in each individual and develops tactics for drawing this out, showing them that they are capable of achieving their desires. This involves being a guide with trusted advice.

- **A helpful and understanding ear:**

  A leader can only be successful if he knows how to listen in a helpful way. A great leader will never punish someone for having concerns or being a bit behind. Instead, he will seek to understand the team member's unique perspective and make sure to always be a helpful presence instead of a domineering one.

- **An adaptable strategist:**

  Being nice and understanding isn't enough. There is a certain level of logic and skill that is necessary to be an effective leader. This means you can realistically assess situations, goals, and the steps for achieving each goal. To be adaptable means, you're capable of looking at the situation and figuring out ways to get to a more ideal place. This involves strategy and openness, as well as a willingness to always be learning.

A healthy coaching session involves a conversation between the authority figure and the person being coached. It focuses on aiding the person being coached to figure out solutions for themselves, based on their own unique reasoning, rather than forcing solutions upon them. Focusing on encouraging independence in finding solutions to and solving problems makes full engagement with methods and material a lot more likely.

Coaching as a Tool for Growth

In many situations, people view the coaching practice as a means for correcting mistakes, to be used only when there's a problem. While this is a useful aspect of the method, coaching is a more positive experience all around when it's used not only as a corrective tool but as an approach for helping people to discover their strengths, identify their ambitions, and set about achieving them effectively.

Deciding on a training course and throwing it at your team members and hoping for the best outcome doesn't always work. Being a coach with a growth perspective involves paying attention to each individual's strengths and bringing them out. It involves being adaptable and listening. Although coaches are not gurus or counselors, many of them borrow methods from professionals in these fields.

Performance Coaching

Performance coaching suggests a new approach to management based on hands-on experience. You, the authority figure, are focusing on the objectives for the team, meaning that the results matter. Focusing too much on the end result, however, can have a detrimental effect. It's all about the development of the full potential of your team, learning to identify and nurture each personality and strength. This involves staying receptive, aware, and innovative.

When you are coaching from a perspective of the ultimate goal, you lose sight of the experience of the journey. You stop seeing individuals, and you start seeing tasks. This disconnects you from the essence of the team and the people within it. Performance coaching requires that you pay attention to what is happening here and now and adjust your style and techniques accordingly.

Coaching Is About Unlocking Potential

For many managers, providing training is just another list item on their busy schedules, and they see team-member development as less important than the tasks they must achieve. What they fail to realize is that they should employ personalized coaching that focuses on unlocking the unique potential in the person. This will create team members who are ambitious and self-assured, resulting in positive results and a huge pay-off for all time invested.

Not only will team goals be more easily accomplished, but it will be a smoother and happier experience for all parties involved and reduce friction and tension. A great leader knows how to create a positive and exciting environment while making sure that his team members stay on track and focused. He is the perfect balance between fun and business and understands that fun is often an important aspect of successful business or tasks of any kind.

The Importance of Having the Right Mindset as a Coach

As a coach or manager, it's important to remember that you are not just trying to instill something specific into someone to get better results. You are unlocking something that already exists within them. It's true that teaching, mentoring, and coaching all share qualities and certain necessary skills, but they are not the same thing, and it's important to understand how. Let's look at some of the key differences between training, mentoring, and coaching.

- **Teaching /Training**:

    Teachers and trainers are given the task of imparting specialized knowledge to a student or students. In this way, teaching is similar to coaching. Although effective teachers are aware of interactive training methods and employ them regularly, there is a clear imbalance of expertise in this dynamic.

    The teacher is assumed to always have the right answers, while the student is just there to absorb the information, as opposed to a coaching relationship where the answers are discovered interactively.

- **Mentoring:**

    In mentoring, there is a general consensus that the mentor is a guiding force who is there to show someone how to achieve things faster than they would on their own. In this way, it is similar to coaching.

Mentoring is different, however, in that the relationship typically focuses on future results, the development of one's career, and broadening horizons for the participant. Coaching has a tendency to focus more on issues that are relevant to the present moment and finding ways to solve them.

- **Teaching and Mentoring vs. Coaching:**

    While a teacher or a mentor is viewed as an expert on the subject at hand, coaching focuses on equipping the individual to discover their unique potential. Rather than the material, the focus lies heavily on the person being coached and what is going on inside of them. A coach is not always someone specifically designated; just about anyone can take this approach including peers or authority figures.

    Instead of the sole focus being on imparting knowledge or skills to a person, the key focus of coaching lies in knowing how to ask the right questions to guide the individual through solving their own issues.

Coaching Is About Helping People Solve Their Own Problems

One method employed by successful coaches is interactively teaching people to follow their instincts. It's not telling the person that you are the sole owner of the right solution and that they must blindly follow you. It's instead teaching them to get in touch with their own potential and learn to get there themselves. Coaches equip people with this ability instead of asking them to submit. Some ways for a leader to help people solve their own issues are:

- **Teaching them to silence their inner dialogue:**

  One way of bringing out these qualities is helping the trainee silence their inner voice. The body knows exactly what to do to achieve great performance; it's just a matter of freeing oneself from the distraction that inner dialogues can cause. In order to effectively help people solve their own problems, removing fear and separating oneself from anxious self-talk is necessary. Once this barrier is removed, the coach can efficiently support the individual's learning process and consequently their overall performance.

- **Helping them identify specific goals:**

  In order to know where you're headed, you must be aware of your own personal goals. A successful coach will help people identify these if they aren't already aware of them. One way to do this is taking some time to think over goals and write them down. A coach can ask his team to think on this and write down three goals for the season and to check in on the status of the goals each week, reviewing and revising as time goes on. At the end of the season, the goals can then be reviewed again and given an assessment.

- **Helping them spot potential roadblocks:**

  To reach your full potential, you must be aware of potential obstacles to success. This means assessing yourself realistically, paying attention to the places you've fallen short in the past, and developing strategies for overcoming similar problems in the future. When a good coach notices a team member making a mistake, he knows the right questions to ask to call attention to this mistake and inspire creative solutions. We will go over these questions later on in the book.

Coaches Drive Results

Being a good coach means you know what to do to achieve the goals of your team. A coach helps the team members identify meaningful, personalized goals and assigns specific behaviors to achieve them. The coach is there to guide and inspire and helps to clarify concrete ways to measure success and maintain motivation. They are also there to hold the members of the team accountable.

On the other hand, a great coach is not obsessed with only results. He or she realizes that they are dealing with real human beings who require different steps and strategies based on their individual skills, abilities, and needs. A successful leader will know exactly how to identify these and draw them out of the people being led.

Coaches Focus on People

Although results are inarguably important and must be focused on to a certain degree, a good coach will never forget that their pursuits are ultimately about people. When you choose who to lead and decide to invest attention in their development, you are making a commitment to helping them grow.

A great leader cannot forget to combine the purpose and the results of coaching to the overall goals. This means they must be aware of what they are, and care enough to adjust courses of action accordingly based on *people* and their needs. They must ask themselves where this is headed, what skills are needed to get there, and always be wondering how they can improve their own leadership techniques. This involves setting strategic leadership goals and ways to measure success in an objective way. This means that they are not only evaluating the team members but also their own effectiveness as a leader of the team.

Someone can be a great coach or leader on paper but have poor interpersonal skills. Great leaders do not just connect with results; they connect to the people and the overall goal of the organization while always remaining open to improvement.

Law Two- Without This Being Strong, You Are Just A Mean Boss

We've all had a mean boss; someone who cared more about numbers and getting things done than creating a harmonious environment in the work place. Efficient coaches know how to avoid coming across this way. They are aware of the importance of creating a strong relationship between themselves and the person they are coaching.

Yelling orders at people and being too rigid is not the way to accomplish this. The relationship must be built on trust and mutual respect for it to be harmonious and healthy. Only then can the team member flourish and accomplish to their full potential.

Simple Ways to Enhance and Build the Person-and-Coach Relationship and Strengthen Respect

Logical leaders who are interested in the pragmatic aspects of achieving goals understand the importance of improving upon and enhancing what already exists within the person being coached. They know that they must be there for the person they are leading. They are more than just a boss or supervisor. They are partners partaking in a relationship between coaches and coached, highly aware of the fact that the coaching dynamic depends upon interaction. The way they listen, take in and reflect upon questions, and provide feedback is all paid attention to and respected. Great coaches are aware of certain techniques that make them effective.

- **Listen Genuinely:**

    Partaking in genuine listening involves being curious about what you're hearing. Every valuable coach knows how to do this, and anyone who would like to become a valuable coach will learn. It's easy to get caught up in tasks and accomplishments and forget to listen with an attentive ear. This type of attitude comes across to the team member and creates discouragement. When a team member comes to you, make sure you're not the one doing all the talking. Be sure to try not to interrupt, while also keeping the topic focused.

- **Absorb What You Hear:**
  It's possible to go through the physical motions of listening and appear on the surface to be paying close attention to what the other person is saying. Even so, you may be too distracted to be absorbing any of it. In addition to seeming genuinely curious, don't neglect making an effort to truly register what they are saying. This is more than just listening to words; you must pick up on gestures, read emotions, and take in the ideas of the other person. This means setting the pace for the conversation and remembering to put yourself in their shoes.

- **Supplying Quality Feedback:**

  Feedback is a word that often has a negative connotation. It's thought of as criticism and nothing else. When employed the right way, however, it can have a very positive affect. Effective coaches know how to go about providing feedback in a way that inspires. They don't use feedback as a way to assert their own authority over the person but instead make sure it's completely relevant and helpful. This makes it a positive exchange.

Perhaps the most important aspect in establishing a healthy coach-team member relationship is the knowledge of how to accurately reflect on information they give you. In addition to the steps outlined above, a great coach should learn this skill to create the optimal dynamic.

How Accurate Reflecting Strengthens Coaching

Accurately reflecting thoughts during a conversation will show the person you're speaking with that you're truly curious and interested in what they're saying. It shows that you have digested what they've put forth. This will also provide an opportunity for them to hear repeated back to them what they had just said and be sure that it accurately represents what they meant. In order to reflect in a positive way:

- **Paraphrase:**

  Paraphrasing involves restating the main gist of something you just heard in your own unique way. It shows that you are listening and absorbing the information, interacting with it in a real way, and not just parroting back what you hear. It shows that you're taking the time to digest the information and hear them out.

- **Summarize:**

  During longer exchanges, you may be taking in a lot of words and information. In this case, knowing how to summarize is a great skill. Oftentimes, a team member will come to you to talk about something and speak in a way that is jumbled, particularly if they are upset. You can help them stay focused and provide some guidance by summarizing.

- **Repeat:**

  Identify which parts of the conversation are the most meaningful, and repeat those words back. This allows the other person to feel heard and understood. It shows them that you are aware of what matters to them and that you're willing to take the time to listen, understand, and help. Also, hearing our own thoughts echoed back to us helps us interact with the knowledge and gain a more objective stance on the matter. This can clear up road blocks and free up mental space for creative solutions.

The Importance of Rewarding Results

Some coaches believe that they must treat everyone the same in order to be fair, but this is how you lose the best members of the team. Exceptional performance deserves to be rewarded. Take the time to compliment people when they do well and institute an incentive system for achievements and high performance. It's not playing favorites; it's acknowledging what deserves to be acknowledged.

It's highly possible to achieve amazing results through instituting a reward system. This will keep people excited about and focused on their goals and achievements. Here are some strategies you can employ:

- **Reward Creative Solutions:**

  Many people, when they are part of a team, simply show up to practice or performances and go through the motions, not bothering to put any heart into it. When someone is interested in and dedicated to the activity, they have suggestions. If a team member takes the time to suggest a solution to an issue or come up with an innovative idea, this deserves recognition and a reward. This will encourage others to strive to do the same thing.

- **Reward Improvements:**

  If someone was falling behind a previous week and suddenly shows a huge spike in stamina or performance, this deserves to be rewarded. Other members of the team will see that improvement gets rewarded and strive to improve their own performance. You can set rewards for different levels of achievement, speed, cleanliness, organization, etc. depending on the organization.

- **Reward Effective Teamwork:**

  Every team, whether it's a team of colleagues, a sports team, or a coordinated dance performance team, needs a harmonious flow and good communication to work together efficiently. If you notice your team displaying signs of communication that pay off with better performance, this deserves recognition as well as some kind of reward. Do not be afraid to comment on great coordinative performance.

Develop Empathy and Rapport

For someone to listen to your input and respect you as a leader, they must feel like you make attempts to understand where they're coming from. Put yourself in the person's shoes and build rapport by making sure you always respect their point of view, ideas, and emotions. To develop empathy and create rapport:

- **Care about the Individuals:**

  You are not just working with numbers or results; these are individuals. If you are leading people, whether it is employees or a sports team, there was a time when you were in their shoes before reaching your point of authority. Place yourself back in that time period to effectively relate to people and receive guidance on how to approach the situation, keeping in mind what they must be feeling and thinking.

- **Speak to Them as Equals:**

  While a teacher sees themselves as the one with the right answers, a coach is more of a partner or a member of the group. Yes, they are learning from you, but you are not just there to impart knowledge or teach them something. You are here to find out which qualities of theirs need to be developed and how. This involves seeing them as equal to yourself, which is the only way you can truly connect with what they need as an individual.

- **Listen with Curiosity:**

  Viewing people you coach as equal's means you listen to what they tell you with genuinely open and curious ears. You are not listening with a harsh and disinterested disposition; you are listening with an intention of figuring out where they're coming from and how best to help them with their needs. This requires staying aware and conscious since that's the only way you can be attentive. What does your body language look like? Are you making eye contact, or staring around distractedly? Are you calmly focused on their speech, or nervously tapping your foot as if you can't wait to get out of there? These are all important cues.

Meet People Where They Are

To be a good coach, you have to be realistic, and this includes meeting people exactly where they are. It may be tempting, in some situations, to get frustrated that the person is not where you believe they should be. In order to fix this, you have to care enough to discover where they're coming from and take the time to meet them in that exact spot. How can effective communication happen if you're trying to communicate from two completely different perspectives? Meeting people where they are means:

- **Asking Instead of Assuming**:

  Say a team member of yours makes a mistake, and you get frustrated. You could be tempted to assume that they weren't listening when you suggested performance techniques to them, or that they are too distracted or don't really care about the situation. Instead of latching onto one of these explanations and making assumptions, you need to remember to ask. This shows that you're willing to find out where they are coming from and meet them halfway.

- **Paying Attention to Emotional Cues**:

  When a person messes up, it could mean that there's something else going on in their lives distracting them. An effective coach realizes this and pays attention to emotional cues. They respond accordingly instead of having a canned response to every situation. They know how to read a person's verbal and nonverbal cues and communicate in a way that will be well-received. This requires a certain measure of emotional intelligence.

- **Taking the Time to Listen and Care:**

   Effective coaches are more than just authority figures; they are trusted guides and partners. They are one of the team memebers. This means that to be an effective coach, you must take the time to listen and care. That means staying aware of your attitude, your questions, and your team members, always. That means keeping yourself in check and always striving to be a better communicator.

If you follow these guidelines, it will be easier for the people you coach to connect with what you say to them. When you take the time to make sure they feel heard and respected, the payoff will be very apparent. When someone has a guide who believes in them and nurtures them in the correct way, they can truly thrive. You may even be surprised at how true this is and how much you yourself can learn and thrive, as well.

Law Three- The Secret to Finding Solutions

The ultimate key to finding great and appropriate solutions is the knowledge of how to ask the right questions.

You must be interactive with your conversations, as a coach. Asking the team member questions allows for a flow of back and forth information and more effective communication.

How Questioning Encourages Exploration:

Helps The Person Find Their Own Solution

Try to focus on open questions as opposed to simple "yes or no" questions. This will give them the chance to find their own answers as well as provide them with practice for doing this in the future. Showing them that they can find their own answers will be an empowering experience for the person. When you ask open questions, this shows that you have faith in their ability to answer. It shows that you respect their opinion, which builds their confidence and performance.

Helps The Person Explore All Aspects of Their Problem

By asking simple "yes or no" questions, you aren't inviting the person talking to expand upon their ideas. You are shortening the conversation and closing doors for a potential learning experience. Asking thoughtful, open-ended questions will ensure that the team member can actively explore each angle of the issue at hand.

Questions Make You a Helper, Not a Boss

Unless you're interested in being a coach solely for the authority it grants you, you should ask thoughtful questions. Consider the concept of asking vs. telling. Simply giving orders to people puts across the idea that you are the one with all the answers and that they are your subordinate. In an effective coaching relationship, the person being coached is an equal participant. This means you ask for their input. Asking questions and helping someone find a solution on their own allows you, as a coach, to be perceived as a helper.

Questions Help to Challenge the Old Thinking and Assumptions of the Person Being Coached

The beauty of conversations is being exposed to new perspectives you've never considered before. Instead of providing them with the answers, you're helping them identify and use their own guidance system. This will show them that they are capable of being independent and innovative and increase their confidence.

Law Four- The Special Ingredient That Makes People Work

A good coach is not a feared authority figure who will make you suffer every time you make a mistake. This type of behavior creates a hostile environment and discourages open, honest communication. To be effective at coaching, you must be an encouraging source of support.

To be Encouraging and Supportive

Coaches Need To Be Good Observers

This involves seeing things in term of the individuals and not just the overall goal. Pay attention to each person's progress and work on development feedback that is relevant to them. Showing that you're paying attention and attentive to their specific personality fosters a healthy partnership where the team member can thrive and perform their best.

Coaches Need to Be Always Focused On Helping the Other Person Reach Their Potential

Each person's potential is a different story, which means a one-size-fits-all approach to coaching is ineffective. Focusing on a specific outcome can lead to neglecting the individual's needs and can lead to a harsh attitude. In order to lead them to their best performance, focus on helping the individual achieve their full potential with careful attention and encouragement.

Coaches Should Give Positive Encouragement Right Away

Harsh, negative criticism fosters an environment of fear and apprehension. If a team member messes up and gets yelled at or punished for it, how likely are they to believe in themselves next time? How likely are they to come to their coach with concerns or issues if they were berated by that person the day before?

A study done by the University of Exeter and published in the Journal of Applied Sports Psychology proved the effectiveness of words of encouragement on athletic performance. Three golfers were given regular words of encouragement and saw a vast improvement in their performance as a result.

Encouragement alone can boost your team's performance. So don't hold back and watch those around you start to improve with just a few simple words of encouragement.

Law Five- The Forgotten Law of Getting Better Results

In order to effectively help team members reach their potential, you must hold them accountable. This means you've made yourself aware of what this person is capable of, and you are making sure they make it there.

Accountability gives the coach permission to help the person accomplish what they desire to accomplish by being honest and straightforward in working towards a goal.

In Order to Effectively Hold People Accountable, You Must

<u>**Decide on a Goal**</u>

Vague and general ideas of wanting to be better are not enough to reach full potential. This requires thought and very specific intentions. Only once someone has pinpointed their goal can they efficiently work toward achieving it. To accomplish things, we must first know what is worth accomplishing, which means deciding on a specific goal.

<u>**Be Clear On Expectations for Both the Coach and Person**</u>

The team cannot reach your expectations if they don't know what they are, just as you cannot perform your duties as a coach without knowing exactly what they entail. Clear communication is of utmost importance for a harmonious environment and optimal performance, both for you and the team.

<u>**Have Set Times to Check In**</u>

Most teams have regular meeting times to review where they are in terms of goals and what needs to be worked on. This not only keeps everyone on the same page and aware of the status of the situation at hand, but having specific times at which to check in and review will also push team members to excel beforehand. Designating times to check in could look like any of the following:

- **A pre-session or pre-practice meeting:**

  This can be a custom that you make a tradition. This meeting could keep fresh in each person's mind exactly what they need to be working on that day, as well as providing tips or advice as to how to achieve those goals.

- **Once a week discussions:**

  Instead of having a meeting before every practice, you can make sure you have one once a week.

Be Honest about Where the Person is by Asking Them Questions

Instead of making assumptions, effective leaders figure out where people are by asking. It's not fair to come at someone assuming that you already know exactly what's going on with them. Approaching the situation in a curious and open manner and discussing the answers is a better method. This will ensure that the person feels comfortable coming to you next time they have a problem, instead of keeping it to themselves. It also provides them with the ability to discover their own answers and learn to believe in them.

Law Six- This is the Only Way for Someone to Get Better

<u>**The Importance of Providing Assessments**</u>

In order to reach goals, it's important to be aware of where you're currently sitting and where you would like to be. Helping a person develop insight about their own self is a key aspect of coaching. This involves providing immediate feedback and helping the team member identify where they want to be and what needs to change in order for that to happen. Providing assessments will:

- **Create motivation and incentive:**

  When someone knows they have an assessment coming up where they will hear in detail all about how they've been performing lately, what needs work, and what they need to do better, they will be motivated to do their best in order to get a better assessment.

- **Maintain discipline:**

  No one likes to be called out and told that they are not doing as well as they could be. Providing regular reviews for your team will ensure that they are trying their hardest because they know that not doing so will be called to their attention.

- **Acknowledge what needs to be acknowledged:**

  Success deserves recognition too. Assessments are not just for criticizing or calling out what needs to be improved upon. Assessments are also there to pay attention to who has been succeeding and why. You could use the person's success as an inspiring example for other members by sharing what they did right in detail.

Assessment involves discussing gaps in performance, inconsistencies, and words vs. action and desires vs. results. You can provide assessments to your team members by checking in with them routinely as they are working toward a goal. This will give you a clear cut image of the direction they would like to head, and you can help them figure out how best to get there.

How to Give Critiques and Positive Criticism

During assessments, your job is to hold the person accountable. This involves being aware of the right methods for providing feedback and critiques. This means communicating to the person exactly what they need to work on in a way that shows them the benefit in doing so. Successful critique is personalized to the person's unique strengths and goals. An important aspect of positive criticism is questions. Here are some examples of questions to open the conversation to critiques.

Inviting and Open Questions:

- **What was your thought process when X happened?**

  Instead of coming at the team member in an accusatory way when they do something that doesn't appear to make sense, try first to find out what was going on in their minds that led up to the occurrence. Not only does this open the door to a healthy understanding exchange, but it allows you to find out exactly what tripped them up, leading you to come up with a valid solution to prevent a recurrence.

- **What is the status of this situation?**

  When a person has an obligation that they have committed to, there is a good way and a bad way to find out how it's going. Asking what the status is of a commitment sounds as though you are neutral in the situation instead of demanding or doubtful. This will lead to a more honest and reciprocal response with a more thorough explanation.

- **Walk me through that error that just happened?**

  This question does not accuse or chastise, but rather presents an air of seeking to understand. You aren't out to make the person feel bad for messing up; you're trying to figure out what caused it. This makes the acknowledgment of the error one of solution-oriented curiosity, and not blame, which will often cause people to clam up.

- **"In what ways can I help you with this?"**

  Asking this shows that you clearly want to help. You are not there to make the person feel worse about a problem, you're there to guide them back to course. As a coach, you are just as interested in them in their success, and this question clearly exhibits that fact. This open-ended question also gives the person the freedom to create their own solution instead of handing them one.

- **"What methods are you going to try next time?"**

This response to an error doesn't focus on the negative aspect of the error; it sees the mistake as a chance to learn. This question shows that you have faith in the person's ability to do better next time, which as a consequence opens the door for them to think in a motivated and creative way about how to improve performance.

- **"How are your thoughts or emotions affecting this?"**

Many times, thoughts or emotions can get in the way of an efficient performance. This can be anything from worry to embarrassment, to something entirely unrelated to the performance itself. Asking this question helps point out the fact that there could be something distracting the person from performing optimally. It calls attention to the effect mental states can have on accomplishing goals. This, in turn, could inspire the person to think of ways to go beyond these distractions when they come up again.

Closed or Interrogative Questions:

- **"Is there a problem here?"**

This question assumes there is something wrong, which could cause a lot of people to freeze up. Focusing heavily on the negative aspect of a situation is likely to prolong it. The question also presupposes that the person being questioned has erred in some way and makes unnecessary assumptions.

- **"Why didn't you do this instead of that?"**

A question like this is full of blame. It assumes that there is one right way to do things and that the person is wrong for failing to perform that specific way. There are many factors that go into mistakes and asking such a question projects the attitude that you are only interested in berating that person's choices and not hearing them out or trying to help.

- **"Didn't I already explain this to you?"**

An unproductive question such as this is full of negativity and hints at the fact that the person you're asking it to doesn't know how to listen or take instruction. The question is not solution-oriented and only comes off as attempting to punish. Instead, you should allow the person to explain their thought processes during the error.

- **"Why did you think that was smart?"**

Again, this is worded very harshly and instantly projects the air that you believe that person is unintelligent or makes unintelligent choices. An accusatory way of asking about a mistake will only make the person feel ashamed and stifle or distract from their performance even more.

- **"Do you really think that will work?"**

Asking this makes it sound as though you disbelieve their idea. It sounds skeptical and negative. If you respond like this to someone's suggestion, it's highly likely that they will start holding back their suggestions out of fear. Instead, seek to understand by asking more questions and trying to get as much information as possible about the situation.

- **"Did you just make that error?"**

When someone messes up, they are usually already very aware of it. To ask this question is to call attention to the mistake itself and not to a solution or understanding. Harsh authority figures call attention to mistakes, while successful, respected coaches only focus on the aspects that can be improved and are not interested in stacking on extra guilt.

Your tone and approach are both extremely important when it comes to feedback. Every signal you give, both verbal and non-verbal, plays a part in how you will be received as an authority figure. In this position, you have a high level of influence that can be intimidating to some, so the tone and words you choose to use are very important. To be more than just a mean boss, learn to word your questions in a positive and open way. People will respond to this and respect you more, and as a result, perform better.

Your Overall Attitude Will Affect:

How Comfortable Team Members Are Bringing Problems to Your Attention

If you're closed off, irritable, and harsh, people will pick up on this and become closed off to you. Instead of knowing that they can come to you for support and encouragement, they will become afraid to open up, fearing a harsh reaction. This will lead to people keeping problems to themselves instead of bringing them to you for help. As a coach, it's your job to be someone that they can come to with concerns, questions, or problems.

How responsive they will be to Your Input

How much we respect a person's opinion has everything to do with the way we perceive that person. If we see our leader as a person to be feared or a grouch that we don't enjoy being around, it's a lot harder to take their words to heart. Even if the words are meant with the best intentions, if they are coming from someone we don't respect or like, they will not be well-received.

How Honest They Will be with You

Not taking the time to communicate respectfully to the people you're coaching means that they won't take the time, to be honest with you. This will mean you are out of sync with them and cannot perform your job effectively. Make sure your attitude is always that of an open and understanding coach.

A non-hostile environment is better for performance of all types because it allows people to relax, flow, and act naturally. Being stiff and worried is a great way to make more errors than you usually would. Creating a relaxed (yet still productive) environment is something every good leader knows how to do. If you aren't aware of it, learn how to do this with the way you interact.

Law Seven- This Skill Keeps Everyone on Track

Communication skills are of utmost importance in a harmonious coaching relationship. In order to help a person reach their full potential, you must know how to reach them. There are some critical questions you can ask yourself to make sure you're staying on track in this area.

Critical Questions for a Coach to Ask Themselves

<u>Do I See and Resolve Conflicts?</u>

Are you present enough to notice conflicts? Am I paying attention to the areas that need work in regards to the team, and constantly assessing the best way to solve these conflicts? Having a serious conversation is not enough to solve every problem. At times, a more formal approach to problem-solving is necessary.

- **Define:**

  First, you must define exactly how performance is not measuring up to expectations. You can only come to a resolution once you know precisely what the issue is in clear and unambiguous terms.

- **Brainstorm:**

  After deciding where expectations are falling short, you come up with some ideas to solve the issue and then establish concrete criteria that will help you to assess these ideas.

- **Analyze:**

  Compare the ideas with each other, reviewing and identifying any potential barriers to resolution. After analyzing the matter carefully, you can come up with a solution that you will test out against your established criteria. This is when you will see what works and what doesn't and redefine ideas as necessary for further testing.

The most important part about this is remaining adaptable. If you see a problem, come up with a resolution, try it out, and if it doesn't work, that just means adjustment is necessary. Remain open to alternatives and always be looking for better ways of doing things. If something isn't working, find another method.

Do I Understand the Difference Between Meaning and Intention?

Earlier, we went over the fact that making assumptions is not a good idea, but one highly important area of communicating effectively as a leader is paying attention to the way you say what you say. This will determine exactly how your thoughts are received by others, how they respond, and whether they are open to listening to you or not.

This means that not only is the meaning behind what you say important, but your tone is too.

It's not Just the Meaning behind What You Say; it's What a Person Hears as Your Meaning

Interactions can be tricky unless you remember the differences between meaning and intention. You may know exactly what thought you're trying to communicate, but whether or not it comes through the correct way depends a lot on the exact words you use. Let's take an example of an employee asking a boss to leave work early. If they ask,

- *"If it's okay, I would like to leave a little early this afternoon. Is that alright with you?"*

This question shows that they genuinely care about whether or not it will be convenient for them to leave early, and they probably really do. However, the person being asked may only hear,

- *"I'm leaving early today whether it's okay or not, and don't care how that affects you."*

In this scenario, the confusion could have been avoided by more thorough expression. For example, it could have been more effective to say,

- *"I would really like to leave work early this afternoon, but if you need to leave as well, I will stay. If me leaving early is alright, can I pay you back by staying late for you sometime next week?"*

Why is being aware of these differences important when it comes to being a coach?

Coaching is about providing help primarily with fostering a supporting and permissive partnership. The coach does not demand or tell people what to do but gets permission first to put forth suggestions. They also seek permission to inquire about matters pertaining to the individual, all while respecting the person they are speaking to. There is a huge difference between asking,

"Is it okay with you if we go to a restaurant to discuss this?

And

"We are going to a restaurant today because it works better than staying on-site."

The first question is phrased in a way that allows the person being asked to decline. The second question states that the asker knows what is best and that they are not open to being swayed. The second option does not show any respect to the team member's opinion and will likely lead to unproductive relationships. For this reason, it's important to remember how you are approaching people being coached. Stay aware of the way you ask things, because every question determines the quality of the relationship and thus the success of your coaching and leadership.

Do I Have a Mission, Vision, or Value Statement?

Having a vision is necessary for being a successful coach. If you don't have a clear mission, it's impossible to be an effective communicator or to accomplish goals. How do you head in the right direction if you don't know which direction it is? Without a vision to keep your sights on, it's too easy for the foundation of your team to crumble. You can start with developing your point of view by thinking about the following questions.

- **Which leaders have impacted you the most?**

  We all have influences that have shaped us in positive ways and inspired us to be our best. It's a great reflection tool to identify which authority figures in your life had the biggest impact and why. This will help you figure out what qualities are the most effective for coaching.

- **What motives you to be a coach?**

  You must identify your purpose in coaching. Without having an idea of what this is, it will be difficult or impossible to stay motivated to fulfill your duties as a leader. If you're not sure what your motivation is, spend some time soul searching and find out.

- **What values are most important to you in coaching?**

  Your values as a leader set the tone for your leadership. What matters most when you're coaching? Is it inspiring people, helping them get organized, helping them calm down and focus? Take some time to figure out exactly what your values are.

- **What can team members expect from you?**

  A good way to make sure you're always being your best and delivering to your team is to identify what they should be able to expect from you at all times. This will help you strive to be the coach you want to be, leading the team to respect your authority, input, and decisions. Find out what team members should be able to expect from their leader so that you can embody that. Ask them what they expect from you as a leader and define it in clear terms so that they can hold you accountable just as you hold them accountable.

- **What do you expect from them?**

  As a coach, it's your job to keep people on course. In order to do this, you must know exactly what your expectations of them are. Take some time to make a list of important expectations, put them into understandable and clear terms, and be sure to communicate this to the people you are coaching. This will set a clear level of communication and prevent misunderstandings.

- **What is your plan for setting a good example?**

  Knowing you want to set a good example is fine, but you need a plan of action. How will you set a great example for your team? How will you set a good leadership model, be a good source of support and be fair in all decision making? These are questions you must ask yourself.

In order to be a great success as a coach and leader, you must reflect on these questions, find out what you value in past leaders, what your purpose is for leading, and what values are the most important to you. To efficiently explore all of these questions you need to:

Write Down Your Questions and Answers

Putting your thoughts into written words will give them more credibility and lasting power. Then, you can take them out every so often, review them and reflect. These can be a great reminder when you're struggling with any aspect of the coaching process or at the beginning and end of seasons.

Find Out When Your Behavior is not aligned with Your Answers

If you are going through a hard time with your leadership, review the answers to the questions above. Oftentimes, when a coach is going through a rough patch, it's because they have lost sight of their vision and are acting in a way that is not in alignment with their answers to those important questions.

Use the Questions to Gain Insight into Your Vision as a Coach

Novice coaches along with veteran ones will be able to use their experiences in asking themselves these questions. The insight they receive from the questions will allow them to reflect on their vision in a meaningful way which provides them irreplaceable insights.

Whichever level you are at in your leadership journey, taking the time to put together a point of view regarding coaching and reflecting on it from time to time will have a huge influence on your team. This method will keep you on track in times of frustration and uncertainty, and remind you why you committed to this journey in the first place.

Some Other Questions to Ask Yourself Consistently

Have I created a motivational environment?

To make sure you're always doing your best as a coach, you must ask yourself whether you are creating an environment that focuses on motivation. Motivation is absolutely mandatory for good results. Your attitude plays a direct role in the team's motivation level. Are you acting open and engaging? How are you coming off to others? Do people seem comfortable when they talk to you? Staying motivated yourself will rub off on the team. Focus on the positive and be sure to bring a lot of positivity and energy to your coaching sessions as well as every interaction you have with members of your team.

How well do I communicate with each person?

Do you feel as though you are communicating effectively with each team member? Are you providing an environment where each person feels comfortable coming to you with any problems? Do you feel comfortable approaching your team members with concerns or questions? Asking yourself these things will tell you what level of communication you're at. In order to effectively improve your communication skills, you can:

- **Ask each person for feedback:**

  Remember that being a coach means fostering relationships and partnerships. This means you need to check in with the people you're coaching to find out how you're doing. Remain open and receptive to suggestions and ways that you can improve your leadership skills. Don't be afraid to ask if you're doing a good job as a coach. This will strengthen rapport and trust because it shows you care enough to ask about how they are doing and what they think. It shows that you respect their opinion and view them as an equal who you can also learn from.

- **Get yourself a mentor or coach:**

  How can you improve as a coach? One great way to become better in this position is getting a coach yourself. Finding a great coach is a way that you can get new ideas. You can acquire new skills to apply to your own leadership. This will also keep you humble in your position of authority since you are also under someone else's guidance. Remember that there is always something you can learn, and a mentor can help you see that. You could also try seeing some of the people you lead as mentors, in a sense, which will help you. This will aid you to stay humble and open to learning from them.

- **Question yourself regularly:**

  We've discussed a fair amount on the importance of questioning your team members and knowing the right ways to do so, but it's also important to question yourself. Having a set list of questions to ask yourself regularly will keep you on track and focused on your vision. Never assume that you don't have more to learn. Leaders can always learn how to lead more efficiently, acquire new tactics, and come up with bigger and better visions for their team. To question yourself regularly means to keep yourself on task and stay in touch with your purpose as a leader

- **Always pay attention:**

  It can be easy to slip into a routine with any repeated behavior and start going on "auto-pilot" when interacting with people. This is a good way to miss important signs or become distracted. Make sure you are always paying attention to your team and what needs to be worked on or addressed. Only then can you achieve what you set out to achieve.

Conclusion

Thank you again for purchasing this book!

I hope this book was able to help give you some ideas on how to be the best coach you can be. Some people are born leaders, and others decide to be one and learn how to assume the position. Regardless of which applies to you, there are principals you can apply to your coaching that will instantly improve its overall quality and efficiency.

Many people have the desire to be a leader and respected authority figure, but to be a truly great one, it takes more effort. You must be adaptable and be aware of how to build healthy, empathetic relationships with the people you coach. With this book as your guide, you should be well on your way to this.

The next step is to work on defining your vision as a coach, start improving your listening skills, and be sure that you ask open-ended questions instead of closed-off ones. Always being aware of your attitude, methods, and impact is crucial to your results.

To be a great leader and coach, remember that people always come first. Although rules, numbers, and results are important, you are always dealing with individuals first and foremost. Getting optimal results depends entirely upon treating them as such and always providing them with respect, hearing them out, and being a source of constant inspiration.

Finally, if you enjoyed this book, then I'd like to ask you for a favor, would you be kind enough to leave a review for this book on Amazon? It'd be greatly appreciated!

Thank you and good luck!

P.S-Don't forget to check out your FREE BONUS on the next page.

Then be sure to continue reading the other books in my "7 Laws" Series on personal development and success. Find all the books on the last page!

FREE BONUS E-BOOK!

Developing Powerful Visions And Inspiring People With Them

Learn how to inspire others with a clear and compelling vision. Understand how to bring your vision to life, and use the wisdom that every great leader has used to help their followers build, maintain and grow their vision into a success!

shapleighpublishing.com/DevelopingPowerfulVisionsBook

OTHER BOOKS IN THE "7 LAWS" SERIES

Check out the current and the upcoming books in Brian Cagneey's "7 Laws" series on personal development and success!

amazon.com/author/briancagneey

The 7 Laws Of Habits: Using Habits To Achieve Success, Happiness, And Anything You Want!

The 7 Laws Of Motivation: Explode Your Motivation And Create A Mindset Built For Success

The 7 Laws Of Happiness: Using The Power Of Happiness To Create Amazing Results In Life!

The 7 Laws Of Productivity: 10X Your Success With Focus, Time Management, Self-Discipline, And Action.

The 7 Laws Of Fear: Break What's Holding You Back And Turn Fear Into Confidence.

The 7 Laws of Confidence: Feel Unstoppable, Destroy Doubt, And Accomplish Your Biggest Goals.

The 7 Laws Of Focus: Focus: The #1 Secret For Excellence, Productivity and Radical Results.

The 7 Laws Of Leadership: Develop Yourself, Influence Others And People Will Follow.

The 7 Laws of Communication: The Secrets Of Being Comfortable, Confident, And Unforgettable With Anyone!

The 7 Laws Of Self-Discipline: Become Strong, Become Confident And Create Your Success

The 7 Laws Of Coaching: Powerful Coaching Skills That Will Predict Your Team's Success

amazon.com/author/briancagneey

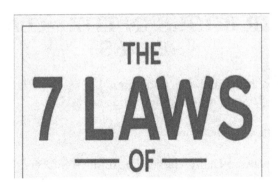

ABOUT BRIAN CAGNEEY

Brian Cagneey is the author of the well-known "7 Laws" book series on personal development. His books cover a wide range of topics including personal growth, habits, self-discipline, happiness, success, communication, leadership, coaching, motivation, confidence, fear, productivity, and focus.

Brian's mission is to renew people's minds and to help every day, ordinary people become positive, successful, and mission driven. His passion for writing is fueled by the desire to see as many people as possible not just survive their life but thrive and excel.

Brian is an avid student of the laws of success. His beliefs on accomplishment are not based on theory, but real life practice. Brian knows that wisdom and knowledge are only half of the equation, the other half of success is taking massive amounts of action over a sustained period of time.

"Anyone can succeed with the ultimate principle of success: small, consistent action over a long period of time. If anyone can master that law through focus, self-discipline and confidence, there isn't anything that's impossible to accomplish."

Check out the other book in the "7 Laws" series today!

amazon.com/author/briancagneey

CPSIA information can be obtained
at www.ICGtesting.com
Printed in the USA
LVHW041444200919
631699LV00017B/205/P

9 781535 389587